David Levinthal

DIE NIBE

Wiener Staatsoper Galerie H.S. Steinek

David Levinthal

LUNGEN

"Dreaming the Middle Ages"

Uns ist in alten Mähren Wunders viel gesagt
von Helden, lobeshehren, von Thaten kühn gewagt;
von frohen Festlichkeiten, von Weinen und von Klagen
von kühner Recken Streiten mögt ihr nun Wunder hören sagen.[1]

JULIEN ROBSON

All of David Levinthal's œuvre has related in one way or another to the American experience and its expression within the cinema: "The West" and "American Beauties" drew upon recognisable aspects of American nostalgia, whilst "Modern Romance" and "Desire" hinted at the darker, more sinister side of 20th Century American culture. Further, it has been noted by Rosetta Brooks that Levinthal's collaboration with Garry Trudeau, "Hitler Moves East", also adresses an aspect of the American experience.[2]

Like all of his previous work Levinthal's new series "Die Nibelungen" is photographed using small scale collector's models within a constructed setting. These tin figures, depicting scenes loosely adapted from the Nibelungenlied, originate in Germany and were manufactured sometime after 1934 by the firm of Werner Scholtz in Berlin.

There is a recognisable shift in the way that Levinthal has photographed these works. Where as in previous series, such as "American Beauties" or "Modern Romance", the figures were deliberately unfocussed, playing upon the duality of the photograph as simultaneously a record of reality and a fiction, these new works focus very clearly upon a sharply defined "dramatis personae", locating them within atmospherically dramatic backgrounds. It is as if the main players, foregrounded in a theatrical set, are captured at key moments within the single stranded narrative of the poem; Kriemhild lamenting over the body of Siegfried; Hagen casting the Nibelungen gold into the Rhine; Kriemhild holding Gunther's severed head vengefully aloft. And yet, whilst they would not look out of place as an accompaniment to the text, there remains something disquieting about the nature of these pictures, an incongruety in their construction that voids their interpretation as mere illustrations and points to their connotative grain, to the questions of representation that

remain a central theme in Levinthal's work.
The Twentieth Century Medieval manifests itself in many ways and in discussing this phenomenon Umberto Eco has referred to Medievalism as being the key to the modern, "the root of all our contemporary 'hot' problems", an era which turned us into "western animals" and amongst whose relics we still live.[3]

As Eco has pointed out, we are in a process of continually reconstructing the Medieval, overlaying it in a way that fits to our present needs, whether as an entertaining distraction, as a way of pondering our current problems or "dreaming, without realising it, of some new reactionary plot". As he further points out, this appropriation is not wholly exclusive to our century and he argues that westerners have been nostalgic for the Middle Ages since Renaissance times.

The hold that popular culture has taken on the Medieval has manifested itself through a collage of fantasy and mythology, where fictional historical or futuristic characters live out heroic roles within scenarios that display all the attributes of the romantic and the chimerical; Dungeons and Dragons proliferate on computer screens; Siegfried and Roy triumph in Las Vegas and Disney conquers Paris, whilst videos, books and comics of heroic knights and distressed maidens abound. Even attempts by Hollywood at fidelity to historical literary material tend to be flawed in order to sustain the market share, overwrought with indulgence and distortions that will guarantee the correct corporate ending. And what all of these manifestations bear in common is the need to invent the present through a re-interpretation of the past, to shroud modern life within the mantle of a dissimulated history.

This "dreaming" of the Middle Ages is of its nature fragmentary, a broken mirror whose shards, when drawn in the name of popular culture, bear no relation to the scholarly study of Medievalism. Rather, it enacts the fantastic against the backdrop of an imaginary past giving scant regard to the representations it engenders and subordinating meaning to effect. From the seeming innocence of Disneyland, our contemporary travels in the Middle Ages have witnessed the advent of Heavy Metal culture, which harnesses the paraphernalia of Medievalism and subjects it to a magic-fantasy-world of misogynistic machismo. Whilst the former veils its corporate intention within the cloak of entertainment, the latter loudly proclaims barbarism as fashion.

Looked at from this perspective, "Die Nibelungen" can be seen as a paradigmatic critique of our fascination with the Middle Ages. Levinthal has welded together two discrepant representations of Medieval mythology; a combination of middle twentieth century German romanticism and the fantastic atmospheric of the Hollywood screen. It is a marriage that is both fragile and highly charged, entangling the indurate and the emotive within the same moment. It seems light, pleasurable, and yet somehow unsettling. Far from collapsing into kitsch, Levinthal's "Die Nibelungen" issues forth questions about the nature of ideology and representation, its seeming innocence opening doors to our understanding of how the apparently naive can be elevated to the point where it is openly oppressive; a poignant observation within our current world politic.

1. "Das Nibelungenlied," translated from Middle High German by
M. Ant. Niendorf, Berlin, 1854.
"We have been told in ancient tales many marvels of famous heroes, of mighty toil, joys, and high festivities, of weeping and wailing, and the fighting of bold warriors - of such things you can now hear wonders unending!"
Translation: A.T. Hatto, The Nibelungenlied, Penguin Classics, 1965.

2. "It seems no accident that this particular work was conceived in the 1970's, a time in America's history when the horrifying reality of the Vietnam War could no longer sustain the fictional realm of war heroism perpetuated by the Hollywood war movies of the 40's and 50's." Rosetta Brooks in "David Levinthal: American Beauties" Catalogue, 1990.

3. Umberto Eco, "The Return of the Middle Ages" in
"Travels in Hyperreality", Harcourt, Brace, Jovanovich, 1986.

Helden des Nordens

Das Epos von den 'Riesenmännern' und den 'Eisenweibern' – eine moderne Geschichte: kalt, grausam, unbarmherzig.

1. Bad girls

„Sie ist ein nettes Mädchen. Nicht mein Typ."
„Sie mögens nicht, wenn sie nett sind?"
„Ich mag böse Mädchen, ausgekocht
und sündenbeladen."

Raymond Chandler: Lebwohl, mein Liebling

ANDREA HURTON

Siegfried und Philip Marlowe? Kriemhild und Chandlers Blondinen mit der Musik in den Hüften?
Das Nibelungenlied - ein film noir?
Was haben das germanische Heldenepos und Hollywoods schwarze Serie miteinander zu tun?
David Levinthal antwortet mit einem Augenzwinkern.
An Mythen fasziniere ihn das Schwanken zwischen Monumentalität und Banalität, hat er einmal gesagt.
Insofern seien der Ring oder die Ilias „monumentale Gesamtwerke", die von „menschlichen Kleinigkeiten" handeln. Letztlich: der bis zum Äußersten getriebene film noir."
In der schwarzen Serie müssen die Charaktere für ihre Sünden bezahlen.
Niemand entrinnt seiner Vergangenheit oder seinem Schicksal.
„Auf uns allen lastet ein Fluch und es ist nur eine Frage der Zeit und der Umstände, bis er ans Tageslicht kommt. Im film noir sind wir dazu verdammt, zu leiden", sagt David Levinthal.
„Ich denke z.B. daran, wie sich Robert Mitchum am Ende von ‚Out of the past' opfert, weil er weiß, daß er, tief in seinem Innersten schlecht ist' und daß sein Ende die einzige Möglichkeit ist, seine Verfehlungen zu rächen. Sein tragischer Fluch war es, sich in die falsche Frau verliebt und ihr geglaubt zu haben."
Und in einer kühnen gedanklichen Volte interpretiert Levinthal Gunther als den schwarzen Helden des Nibelungenlieds: seine obsessive Passion, Brunhilde zu besitzen, sei in Wahrheit die tragische Verfehlung, die unaufhaltsam in den Abgrund führt. Brunhilde hetzt Gunther auf: um ihre Schmach zu tilgen, muß Siegfried bezahlen.
Die einzig interessanten Frauenfiguren hier wie dort, im film noir und im Nibelungenlied, sind die „bad girls".

Die Blondinen mit den roten Mündern und dem Gang, den man ihnen nicht auf der Handelsschule beigebracht hatte; Kriemhild, die Rächerin, deren Handeln nur von niedrigen menschlichen Regungen wie Eifersucht und Stolz beherrscht wird. Der Streit der Königinnen löst die unaufhaltsame Tragödie aus. Wie im Plot eines klassischen misogynen film noir, ist es auch im Nibelungenlied die Verfehlung einer Frau, die die tödliche Lawine ins Rollen bringt.

Unter der ritterlichen Patina des Nibelungenlieds schimmern die wilden, archaischen Grundzüge des Stoffes durch. Die Welt ist schlecht, und ihre Bewohner verhalten sich zueinander wie die wilden Tiere. So ragt tiefstes Mittelalter in unsere aufgeklärte Gegenwart hinein.
In Levinthal's Arbeiten, so entrückt ihre Themen scheinen mögen, spiegelt sich immer ein Bild von Amerika.
Die Sehnsucht der modernen amerikanischen Gesellschaft nach den einfachsten Lösungen für politische und soziale Probleme, die Worthappen, die die Politiker dem Stimmvolk zuwerfen, das ist für Levinthal die Brücke von der brutalen Archaik des Nibelungenlieds zu unserer subtiler, aber letztlich nicht minder gewalttätigen modernen Gesellschaft. Wo enden Bestrafung und Rache und wo beginnt das Böse?
Levinthal vergleicht Kriemhilds pervertierten Rachegedanken mit dem fanatischen Gerechtigkeitswahn amerikanischer Abtreibungsgegner, „die glauben, es ist in Ordnung, wenn man einen Arzt tötet, um das Leben des ‚Ungeborenen' zu retten. Es sind diese Emotionen und Gefühle, die sich von den Nibelungen bis zu uns nicht wirklich verändert haben."

2. Die Spielzeugfiguren machen uns zu Göttern.

David Levinthal's Obsession sind Mythen. Sie sind für ihn Ikonen und Metaphern, sie bringen das Wertesystem einer Gesellschaft auf den kleinsten Nenner. Er hat sich mit ganz unterschiedlichen Themen beschäftigt - mit tapferen Cowboys, wilden Indianern, hüftschwingenden Schönheitsgöttinnen oder jetzt in den Nibelungen mit betrogenen Helden und rachedürstigen Frauen.
Aber dabei hat er immer die Doppelbödigkeit und die Mehrdeutigkeit gesucht. Der einfachen Lesart, die den Betrachter bei der Hand nimmt und ihm ein spannungsloses, völlig zu Ende gedachtes Bild zeigt, hat er sich verweigert.
Auch „Die Nibelungen" sind schillernd in ihrer Vieldeutigkeit. Sie sind vieles zugleich: opernhafter Hintergrund – Ikonen des Heldentums – ironischer Kommentar einer politisch mißbrauchten Symbolik. Deswegen photographiere er Spielzeugfiguren, sagt Levinthal. Sie lassen es zu, daß wir unseren Gedanken freien Lauf lassen und „unsere eigenen Gefühle projezieren. Die Spielzeugfiguren machen uns zu Göttern."
Die Zinnfiguren, die die Helden seiner Nibelungenserie sind, hat er 1991 in Berlin bei einem seiner Streifzüge durch Antiquitätengeschäfte gefunden. Sie stammen wahrscheinlich aus dem Jahr 1934 und sind eine Kreuzung aus Nibelungenmythos, einer Prise Wagner und „arischer Tugend".
„Es besteht eine offensichtliche Verbindung zwischen der Zeitperiode, als diese Figuren für die Gußformen geschaffen wurden und den politischen und sozialen Zielen dieser Epoche. Damals gab es viel „heroische arische Kunst" - ich denke an Gemälde Hitlers, wo er eine Rüstung trägt und eine Lanze (wie Siegfried vielleicht?)."
So wie in seiner ersten Arbeit mit dem Titel „Hitler Moves East" rührt Levinthal auch mit den Nibelungen an ein politisch sensibles Thema, dessen Brisanz sich noch dadurch verschärft, daß der Künstler jüdischer Abstammung ist. Aber Levinthal läßt sich durch die vorbelasteten Themen nicht zu zwanghafter Didaktik oder akademischer Verkrampfung hinreißen. Auch die Tatsache, daß er Jude ist, sieht er nicht in direktem Zusammenhang mit seinen zum Teil auf germanisches Heldentum bezogenen

Themenstellungen. „Das sind meine teutonischen Wurzeln", hat er dazu einmal scherzhaft gemeint.
Die visuellen Effekte der Nibelungenserie hat Levinthal auf folgende Weise erzielt: er stellt die Figuren auf eine einfache Grundlage, Sand oder ein anderes Schüttmaterial und bedeckt ihren Sockel. Als Hintergrund verwendet er Elemente und Gebäude, wie sie bei Spielzeugeisenbahnen verwendet werden.
„Manchmal wollte ich, daß der Hintergrund sichtbar bleibt, z.B. als ich die Ruine des Schlosses oder den roten Triumphbogen verwendete. Dann wieder wollte ich einen in seinen Konturen und Farben völlig abstrakten Hintergrund, z.B. auf dem Bild von Hagen und Gunther oder auf dem Photo von den Rheintöchtern mit dem farbigen Hintergrund."
Das Licht und die Farbe auf den Figuren sind zumeist Reflexionen der Farben des Hintergrundmaterials.
Wenn Kriemhild Gunthers Kopf in der Hand hält, ist sie ganz in Rot getaucht, in ein Rot wie Blut, das vom Rot des Schlosses im Hintergrund vom Sand auf die Figur reflektiert.
Diese Bilder sind sehr theatralisch. Zum Teil wegen ihres Gegenstandes, zum Teil durch die Art und Weise, wie Levinthal sie photographiert hat. Anders als in fast allen seinen früheren Arbeiten, stehen die Figuren im Zentrum. Man kann ihren Spielzeugcharakter deutlich erkennen. All das trägt zum dramatischen Gehalt dieser Bilder bei. Sie sind Theater.

Illetschko, Peter. "Fabrik der Mythologien," Der Standard, May 8, 1992, Sec.A, p.10.

"Imaged Documents," C.E.P.A. Quarterly, Winter/Spring 1988, pp.15-17.

Kessler, Pamela. "The Created Event," The Washington Post, March 26, 1988, p.C2.

Knight, Christopher. "Photographer Levinthal Goes West," Los Angeles Herald Examiner, April 14, 1989 Weekend, p.4.

Levinthal, David and Garry Trudeau. "Hitler Moves East: A Graphic Chronicle 1941-43," New York; Sheed, Andrews & McMeel, 1977.

Levinthal, David. "Captain Gallant," American Art, Winter/Spring 1991, Volume 5, No.1-2, pp.60-67.

Levinthal, David. "Hitler Moves East," Camera Austria 33/34, 1989, pp.49-56.

Levinthal, David. "Modern Romance," Aaron Press, in Association with Founders Gallery, University of San Diego, 1985.

Murray, Joan, "Memorable Books," Artweek, January 7, 1978, pp.13-14.

Pagel, David. "David Levinthal," Art issues, September/October 1989, p.28.

Robson, Julien. "Interpreting The American Dream," Graz; Galerie Eugen Lendl, 1992.

Solomon-Godeau, Abigal. "In Plato's Cave," New York; Marlborough Gallery, 1983.

Solomon-Godeau, Abigal. "Photography at the Dock," The Art of Memory / The Loss of History, New York; The New Museum of Contemporary Art, 1985.

Starenko, Michael. "Modern Romance," Afterimage, January 1986, p.21.

Storr, Robert. Devil on the Stairs, Institute of Contemporary Art, Philadelphia, 1991.

Sullivan, Constance. Ed. "The Wild West," Washington D.C. and London Smithsonian Institution Press, 1993.

Sultan, Terrie. "Surrogate Selves: David Levinthal, Cindy Sherman, Laurie Simmons," Washington D.C.; the Corcoran Gallery of Art, 1989.

Thorson, Alice. "Camera Records Invented Worlds," The Washington Times, April 21, 1988, p.E3.

Weiley, Susan. "The Darling of the Decade," ARTnews, April 1989, pp.143-150.

Wise, Kelley. "Photos Miniature the Old West," The Boston Globe, February 13, 1988, p.24.

Woodward, Richard B. "David Levinthal," ARTnews, March 1989, p.108.

Woodward, Richard B. "Taking Toys Seriously: Mini-Movement or Sideshow," The New York Times, February 26, 1989, Sec. 2, pp.39-40.

Acknowledgements

This catalogue has been produced to coincide with the first showing of David Levinthal's "Die Nibelungen" in the Marmorsaal of the Vienna State Opera, May 1993.

Thanks are due to Dr. Monika Faber of the Österreichisches Fotoarchiv and Ernst Kapplmüller for their initial enthusiasm and assistance in developing this project. Credit is also due to Dr. Georg Springer and Frau Mag. Angelika Dwořak of the Österreichischer Bundestheaterverband for their commitment to the exhibition and assistance in its realisation. Finally we would like to thank Ronald Post, Cultural Attaché at the United States Embassy and Mumm & Co Sekt for their additional support.

Galerie H.S. Steinek

Published by/Herausgeber
Galerie H.S. Steinek
Himmelpfortgasse 22
A-1010 Wien

Translations/Übersetzungen
Werner Rodlauer

Design/Gestaltung
Alan Moore

Print/Druck
Graphische Kunstanstalt
Otto Sares GmbH, Wien

„Das Mittelalter träumen“

Uns ist in alten Mähren Wunders viel gesagt
von Helden, lobeshehren, von Thaten kühn gewagt;
von frohen Festlichkeiten, von Weinen und von Klagen
von kühner Recken Streiten mögt ihr nun Wunder hören sagen[1]

JULIEN ROBSON

Das gesamte Oeuvre von David Levinthal bezieht sich in der einen oder anderen Weise auf die „Amerikan Experience“ und ihre Umsetzung im Film: „The West“ und „American Beauties“ befaßten sich mit erkennbaren Aspekten amerikanischer Nostalgie, während „Modern Romance“ und „Desire“ auf die dunklere und unheilvollere Seite der amerikanischen Kultur des 20. Jahrhunderts hinwiesen. Auch Levinthal's Zusammenarbeit mit Garry Trueau - „Hitler Moves East“ - weist laut Rosetta Brooks auf einen Aspekt des Lebens in Amerika hin.[2]

Wie in allen seinen vorhergehenden Arbeiten photographierte Levinthal seine Serie „Die Nibelungen“ indem er kleine Spielzeugfiguren in einer konstruierten Szenerie verwendet. Diese Zinnfiguren, die Szenen nach Vorlagen aus dem Nibelungenlied zeigen, stammen aus Deutschland und wurden einige Zeit nach 1934 in der Manufaktur von Werner Scholtz in Berlin gefertigt.

Die Art wie Levinthal diese Arbeiten photographiert hat, macht eine Abweichung in seiner Arbeitsweise erkennbar. Während in früheren Serien wie „American Beauties“ oder „Modern Romance“ die Figuren absichtlich unfokussiert waren und so auf die Dualität der Fotographie als Fiktion und Abbild der Wirklichkeit anspielten, richten sich diese neuen Arbeiten sehr klar auf genau definierte Handlungsträger und stellen sie in ein atmosphärisch-dramatisches Umfeld. So als ob die Hauptdarsteller, wie vor ein Bühnenbild gestellt, in Schlüsselszenen gefangen wären, während das Gedicht den Handlungsfaden weiterspinnt; Kriemhild, wehklagend über dem Leichnam von Siegfried; Hagen, der das Gold der Nibelungen in den Rhein wirft; Kriemhild, die Gunthers abgetrennten Kopf rachevoll hochhält. Auch wenn sie nicht deplaziert wirken als Illustration zum Text, so liegt doch etwas Beunruhigendes in der Erscheinung dieser Bilder, eine Ungereimtheit in ihrer Konstruktion, die ihre Interpretation als reine Illustration verweigert und auf ihren konnotativen Grundgehalt verweist, die Frage nach der Repräsentation, die das zentrale Thema in Levinthal's Arbeit bleibt.

Das „Mittelalter im 20. Jahrhundert" manifestiert sich auf vielfache Weise. In der Diskussion dieses Problems verwies Umberto Eco darauf, daß das Mittelalter der Schlüssel zur Neuzeit sei, „die Wurzel all unserer gegenwärtigen ‚heißen' Probleme", eine Ära, die uns in „abendländische Tiere" verwandelt hat und in deren Relikten wir noch immer leben.[3] Eco hebt hervor, daß wir das Mittelalter noch immer neu konstruieren. Wir passen es lediglich unseren gegenwärtigen Bedürfnissen an. Sei es als unterhaltende Zerstreuung, die Art wie wir unseren Problemen begegnen, oder ob wir „ohne es zu wissen, einen reaktionären Plan aushecken". Weiter zeigt er, daß diese Aneignung nicht ausschließlich unser Jahrhundert betrifft. Seit der Renaissance, so Eco, hing der Westen einer Nostalgie nach dem Mittelalter nach.

Daß auch die populäre Kultur das Mittelalter vereinnahmt, zeigt sich an der Collage von Fantasy und der Mythologie, in der fiktionale historische oder zukünftige Charaktere ihre Heldenrollen in einer Szenerie erleben, die alle Attribute des Romantischen und der Chimäre trägt. Verliese und Drachen bevölkern die Computerbildschirme; Siegfried und Roy feiern Triumphe in Las Vegas und Disney erobert Paris, während es von Videos, Büchern und Comics mit heroischen Rittern und bedrängten Fräulein wimmelt. Sogar Hollywoods Versuche der Werktreue gegenüber den historischen Vorlagen erscheinen verfälscht um den Marktanteil zu halten - überfrachtet mit Gefälligem und Verzerrtem um das den Produzenten genehme Ende zu garantieren. Allen diesen Erscheinungen gemein ist die Sucht, die Gegenwart durch eine Re-Interpretation der Vergangenheit neu zu erfinden und das Leben heute unter dem Deckmäntelchen einer umgeschriebenen Geschichte zu verstecken.

Dieses „Träumen" des Mittelalters ist in seiner Struktur fragementarisch, ein zerbrochener Spiegel, dessen Splitter, im Lichte der Populärkultur gesehen, nichts vom gelehrsamen Studium des Mittelalters zeigen. Sie stellen eher das Phantastische vor dem Hintergrund einer erfundenen Vergangenheit dar, nehmen wenig Rücksicht auf die Vorstellungen, die sie vermitteln und ordnen die Bedeutung dem Effekt unter. Ausgehend von der scheinbaren Unschuld Disneylands haben wir auf unseren gegenwärtigen Ausflügen in das Mittelalter das Erscheinen der Heavy Metall Kultur erlebt, die mittelalterliche Requisiten vereinnahmt und sie einer magischen Fantasy-Welt voll misogynem Machismus zuordnet. Während erstere ihre wirtschaftlichen Absichten mit dem Schleier der Unterhaltung umgibt, erklärt letztere lauthals den Barbarismus zur Mode.

Aus dieser Sicht kann „Die Nibelungen" als eine exemplarische Kritik an unserer Faszination vom Mittelalter gesehen werden. Levinthal hat zwei gegensätzliche Bilder der Mittelalterlichen Mythologie vereinigt - den Romantizismus Deutschlands in der Mitte des 20. Jahrhunderts und die phantasievolle Atmosphäre des Hollywood-Kinos. Es ist eine Verbindung, die fragil und äußerst gespannt ist, die Abstumpfung und Erregung gleichermaßen verknüpft. Sie erweckt Leichtigkeit und Freude und mündet doch in Unbehagen. Weitab von der Gefahr dem Kitsch zu verfallen, stellt Levinthal's „Die Nibelungen" die Frage nach der Herkunft von Ideologie und Bild und ihre scheinbare Unschuld öffnet unserem Verstand die Türen um zu verstehen, wie offensichtliche Naivität zu einem Punkt gelangen kann, an dem sie zur unverhüllten Tyrannei wird - eine scharfsinnige Beobachtung in unserer gegenwärtigen politischen Landschaft.

1 „Das Nibelungenlied", aus dem Mittelhochdeutschen übertragen von **M. Ant. Niendorf, Berlin 1854**

2 „Es erscheint kaum als Zufall, daß diese Arbeit in den 70ern geschaffen wurde. Zu einem Zeitpunkt in der Geschichte Amerikas, an dem die Fiktion des Kriegs-Heldentums, wie es in den Kriegsfilmen Hollywoods der 40er und 50er Jahre immer dargestellt worden war, der schrecklichen Wahrheit über den Vietnamkrieg nicht mehr standhalten konnte."
Rosetta Brooks, „David Levinthal: American Beauties", Katalog, 1990

3 Umberto Eco, „The Return of the Middle Ages" in:
„Travels in Hyperreality" ,Harcourt, Brace, Jovanovich, 1986

Northern Heroes

The Epic of "Ogre Men"
and "Iron Ladies "-
a Modern Story:
Cold, Cruel, Unforgiving

ANDREA HURTON

1. Bad Girls

"She is a sweet girl. Not my type."
"You don't like it if they are nice?"
"I like the bad girls, tricky and wicked."
Raymond Chandler: Goodbye My Dear

Siegfried and Philip Marlowe? Kriemhild and Chandler's blondes with music in their hips? The Nibelungenlied - a film noir? What does this germaic heroic epic and Hollywood's 'serie noir' have in common? David Levinthal answers with a wink. He once said that the oscillation in myths between monumentality and banality had always fascinated him. And in this respect the Ring or the Iliad represent "monumental œuvres" dealing with "human bagatelles", the ultimate film noir. In film noir the characters have to pay for their sins. Nobody could escape one's past or one's fate. "There is almost an assumption that we are all flawed in some way, and that it is only a matter of time and circumstances before that flaw is revealed. In 'noir' it seems that we are all made to suffer", as David Levinthal puts it. "I think of Robert Mitchum sacrificing himself at the end of 'Out of the Past', because he knows that 'deep down' he is no good and that his end is ultimately fair and the only way to right all his previous wrongs. His tragic flaw was in falling for the wrong woman and then believing her." Then in a daring volte-face Levinthal defines Gunther as the black hero of the Nibelungenlied; his obsessive passion to possess Brunhilde being his tragic undoing, leading irresistibly into the abyss. Brunhilde taunts Gunther and to expiate her disgrace Siegfried has to pay. The only interesting women characters here, both in film noir and the Nibelungenlied, are the bad girls, the blondes with the red lips and a gait which could not have been picked up at secretarial college. Kriemhild the avenger whose behaviour is dominated by low human emotions such as jealousy and pride. The feud between the queens engenders the inexorable tragedy.

As in the plot of a classic misogynistic film noir, so in the Nibelungenlied, it is the fault of a woman that sets the deadly avalanche rolling.
Beneath the Chivalric patina of the Nibelungenlied the wild and archaic roots of the story are shining through. The world is bad and it's inhabitants behave like ferocious animals. So, the deepest Medieval penetrates our enlightened present.
Yet, however distanced their subject may be, there is always the image of America in Levinthal's works.
For Levinthal, it is the longing of modern American society to find the most simple solution for political or social problems - the sound bites which politicians toss at the electorate - which builds the bridge between the cruel archaic of the Nibelungenlied and our subtle but finally no less violent modern society. Where does punishment and revenge end and evil begin?
Levinthal compares Kriemhild's perverted spirit of revenge with the fanatic mania for Justice of American anti-abortion people, those "that feel it is alright to kill a doctor because they are saving the lives of the 'unborn'. It is these types of emotions and feelings that have not really changed that much from the Nibelungenlied till now."

2. With toys we are Gods

David Levinthal's obsession is myths. To him they are icons and metaphors, they reduce a society's values to a common denominator. He has dealt with very different issues - brave cowboys, wild Indians, hip-swinging beauty queens - or as now, in the Nibelungen, victimized heroes and vindictive women.
But he has always searched for equivocality and ambiguity, always voided the easy reading which takes the reader by the hand and shows him a suspenseless fully visualized image.
The Nibelungen are dazzling in their ambiguity. They are manifold; operatic background - icons of heroism - ironic comment on a politically abused symbolism.
This is why he photographs toy figures, Levinthal says. They let our thoughts take their own course and "let us project our own feelings. With toys we are gods."
He found the tin figures, the heroes of the Nibelungen series, in Berlin in 1991 during his strolls through antique shops. They date from around 1934 showing a combination of Nibelungen mythology, some Wagnerian elements and "Aryan virtues".
"There is an obvious connection between the time period when these figures were sculpted for molds and the political and social aims of the period. There certainly seemed to be a lot of 'heroic Aryan art'. I think of the paintings of Hitler on horseback wearing a suit of armor and carrying a lance (like Siegfried perhaps?)"
As in his first work, "Hitler Moves East", Levinthal's "Die Nibelungen" touches upon a politically sensitive issue whose explosiveness is fuelled by the fact that the artist is of Jewish descent.
But these loaded issues do not drive Levinthal into didactic rationalisations or academic cramps. Neither does he see the fact that he is Jewish being directly influencial upon his use of themes relating to germanic heroicism.
"These are my teutonic roots" he once said jokingly.
Levinthal gained the visual effect in the series "Die Nibelugen" by the following: He sets the figures up on a simple ground, sand or other material covering the figure's bases. To create a background he uses elements and buildings used for model railroads.

“Sometimes I would want the background to remain somewhat visible, such as when I used a ruined castle or the red archway. Other times I wanted the background to be completely abstract, such as when I had Hagen and Gunther standing together, or the picture of the Rhine maidens with the color background.”
Most of the light and the colour on the figures are reflections of the colours of the background materials. Thus Kriemhild holding Gunther’s head has a red colouring like blood, which is reflected from the castle behind onto the figure, by the sand in front.
These images are very theatrical, partly due to their theme as well as the way Levinthal has photographed them. Different from most his earlier works, the figures form the centre. One can easily perceive their toyness. All of this adds to the dramatic content of these pictures:
They are theatre.

1. Siegfried's armour
Siegfrieds Rüstung
Cibachrome print
1993

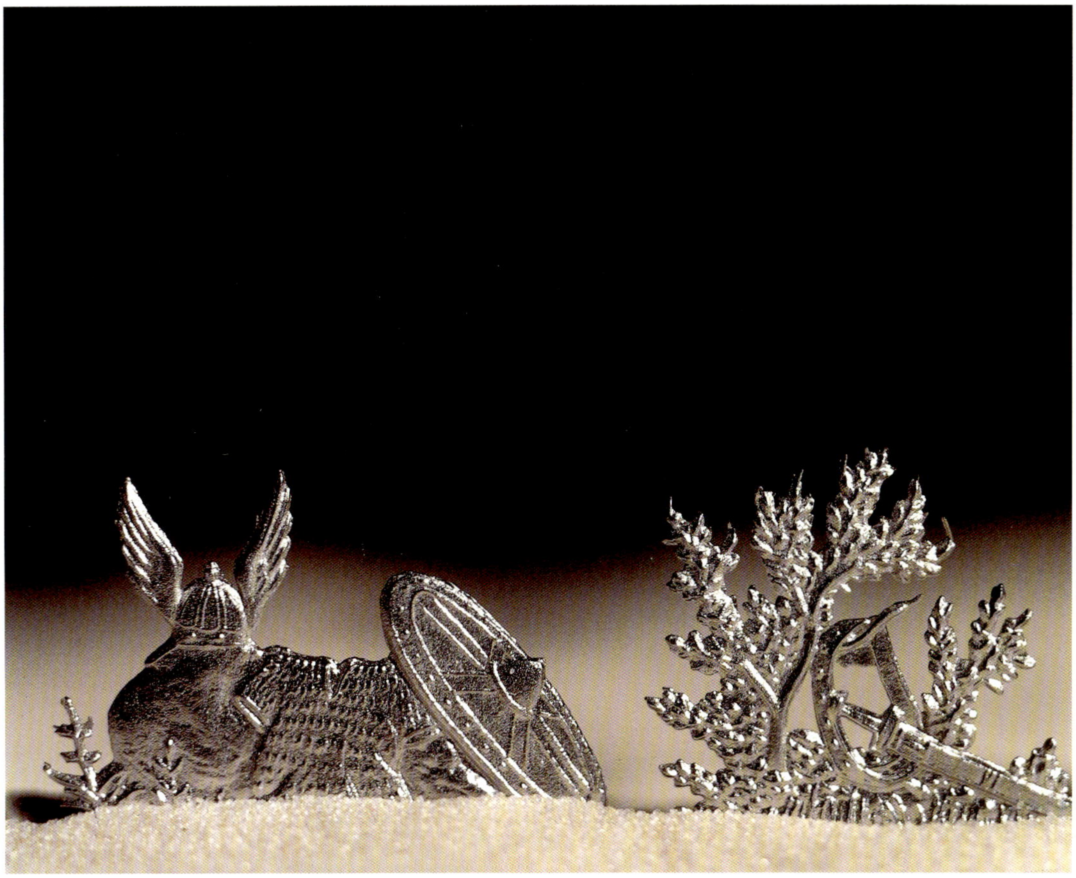

2. Siegfried's death
Siegfrieds Tod
Cibachrome print
1993

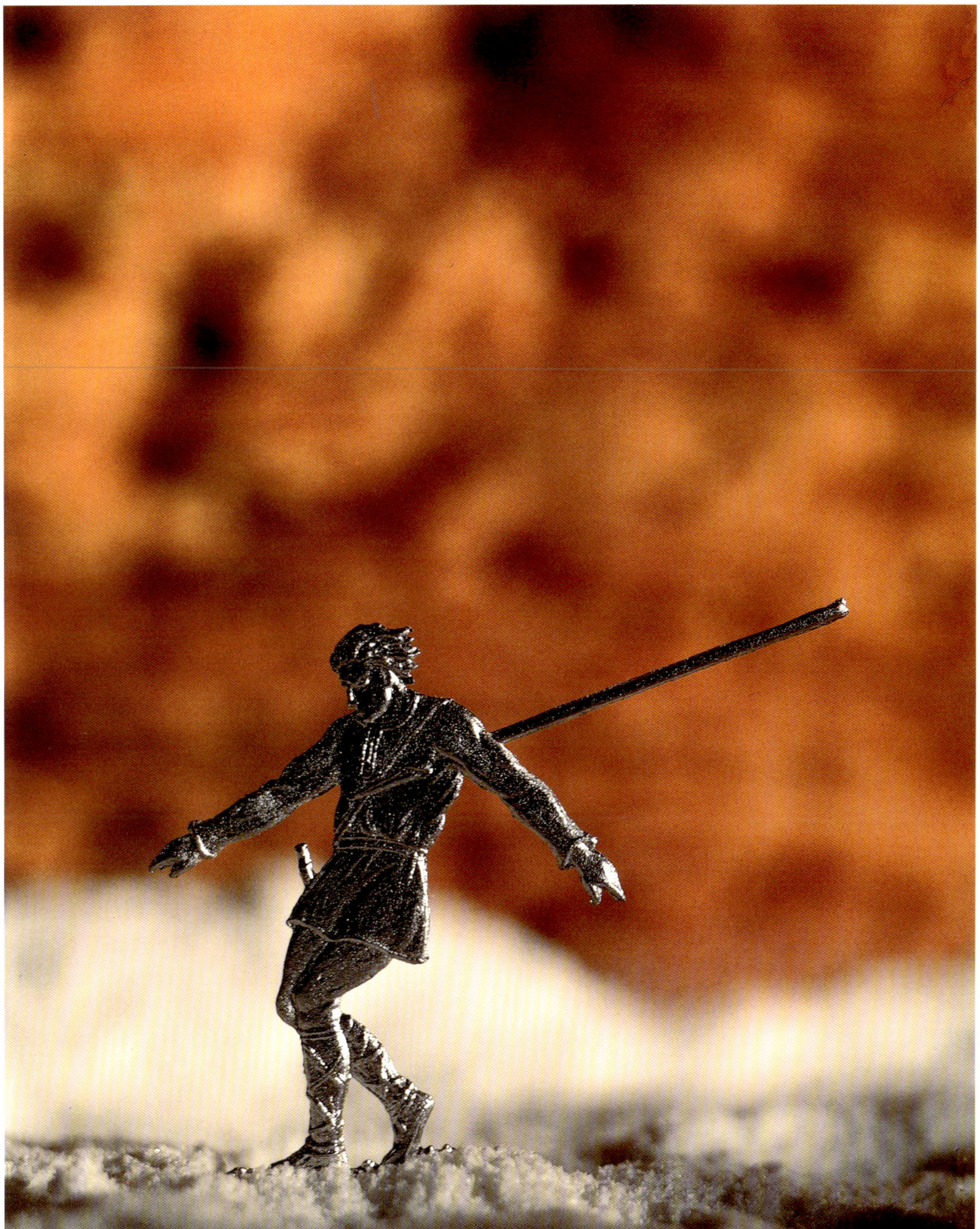

3. Kriemhild at Siegfried's funeral bed
Kriemhild an Siegfrieds Totenbett
Cibachrome print
1993

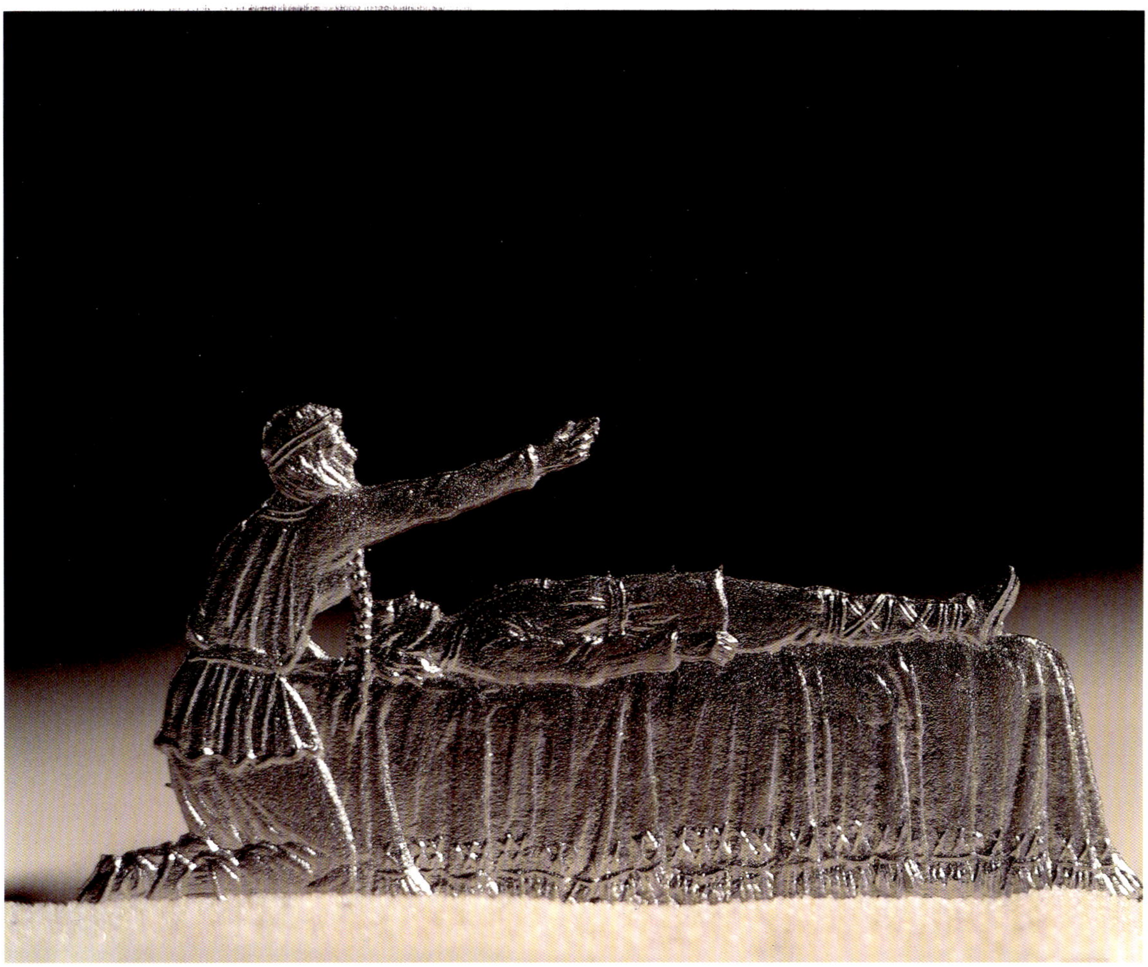

4. Kriemhild mourning in Worms
Kriemhild trauert in Worms
Cibachrome print
1993

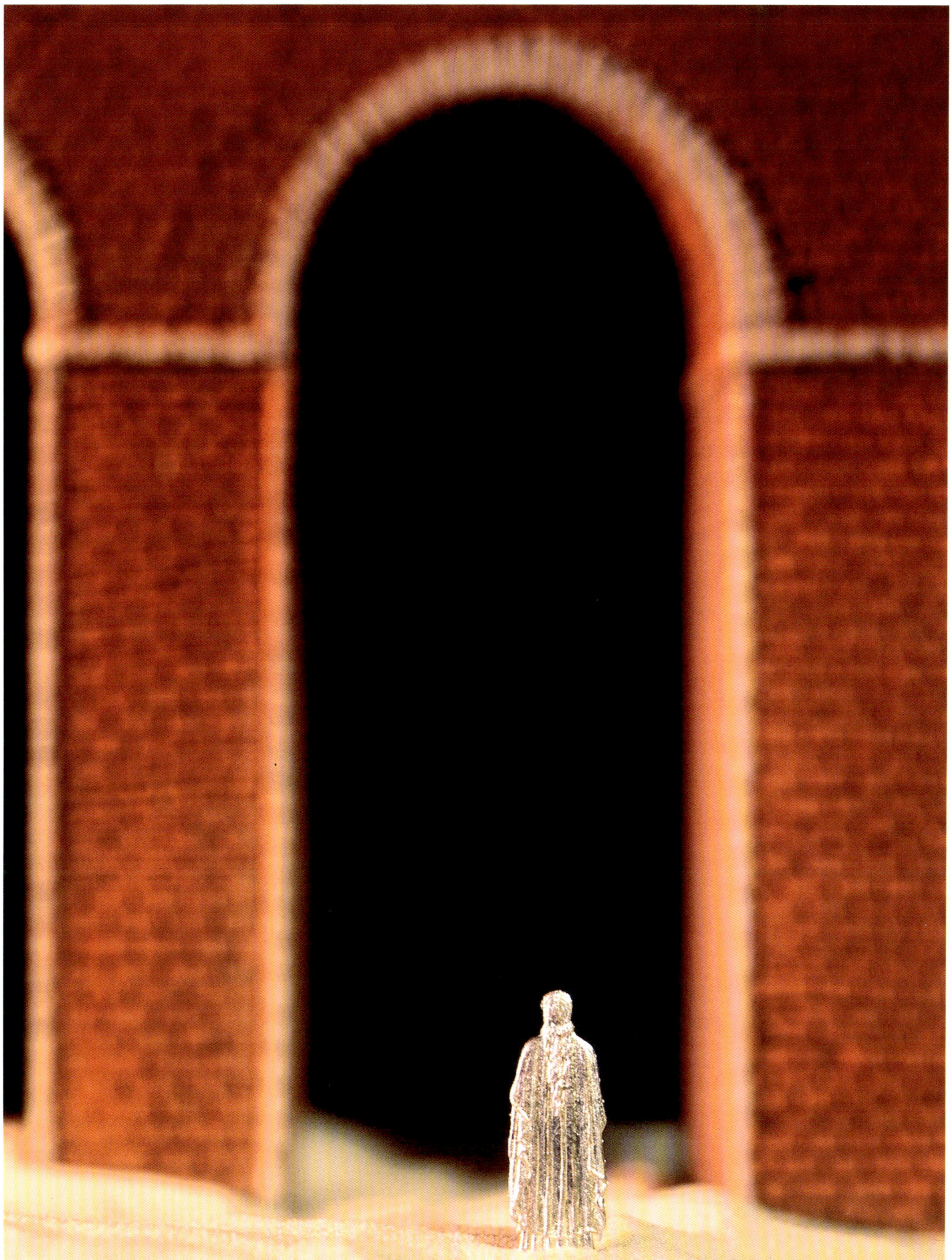

5. Hagen casting the Nibelungen
treasure into the Rhine
Hagen wirft den Schatz
der Nibelungen in den Rhein
Cibachrome print
1993

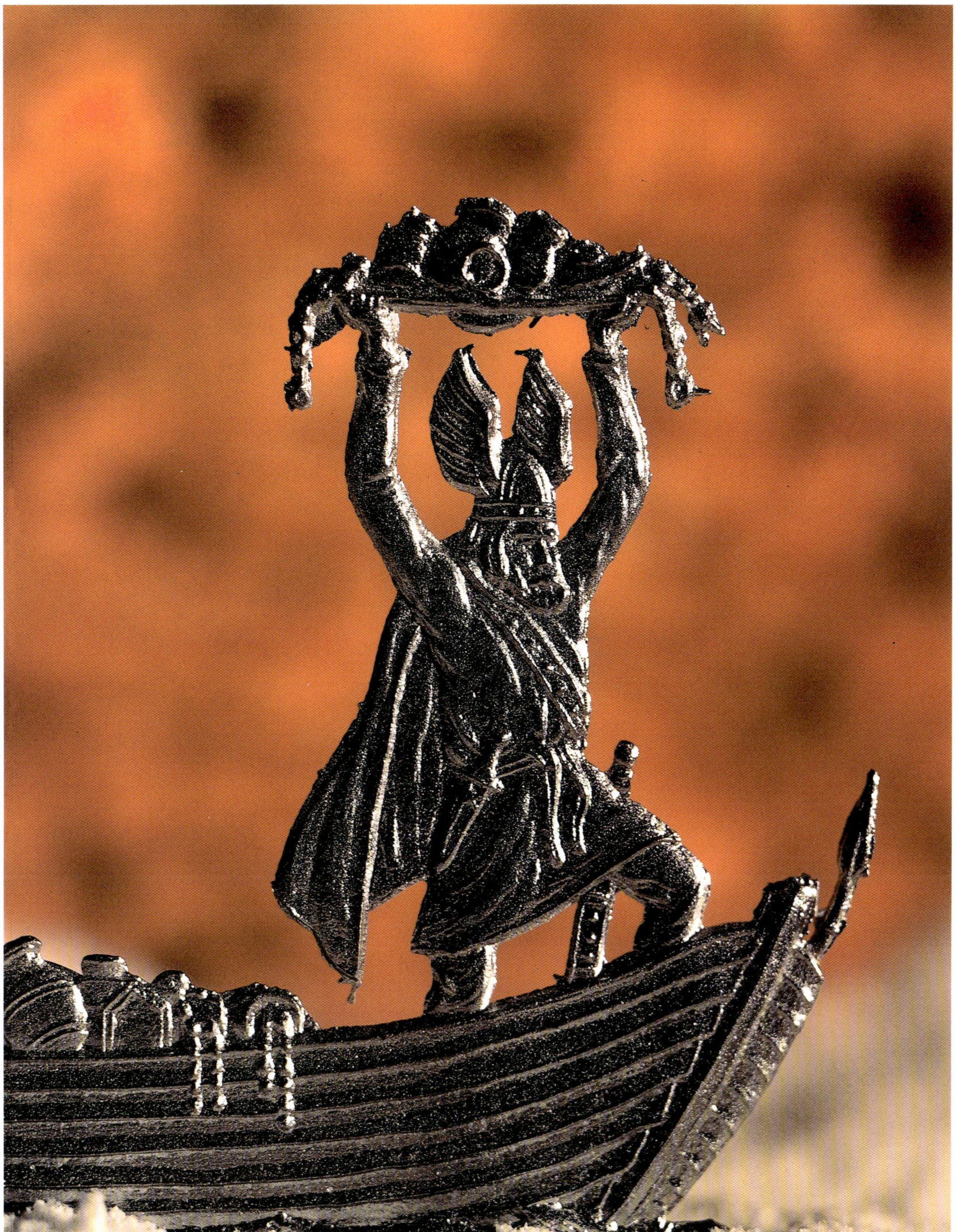

6. Kriemhild entering Etzel's land
Kriemhild kommt in Etzels Reich
Cibachrome print
1993

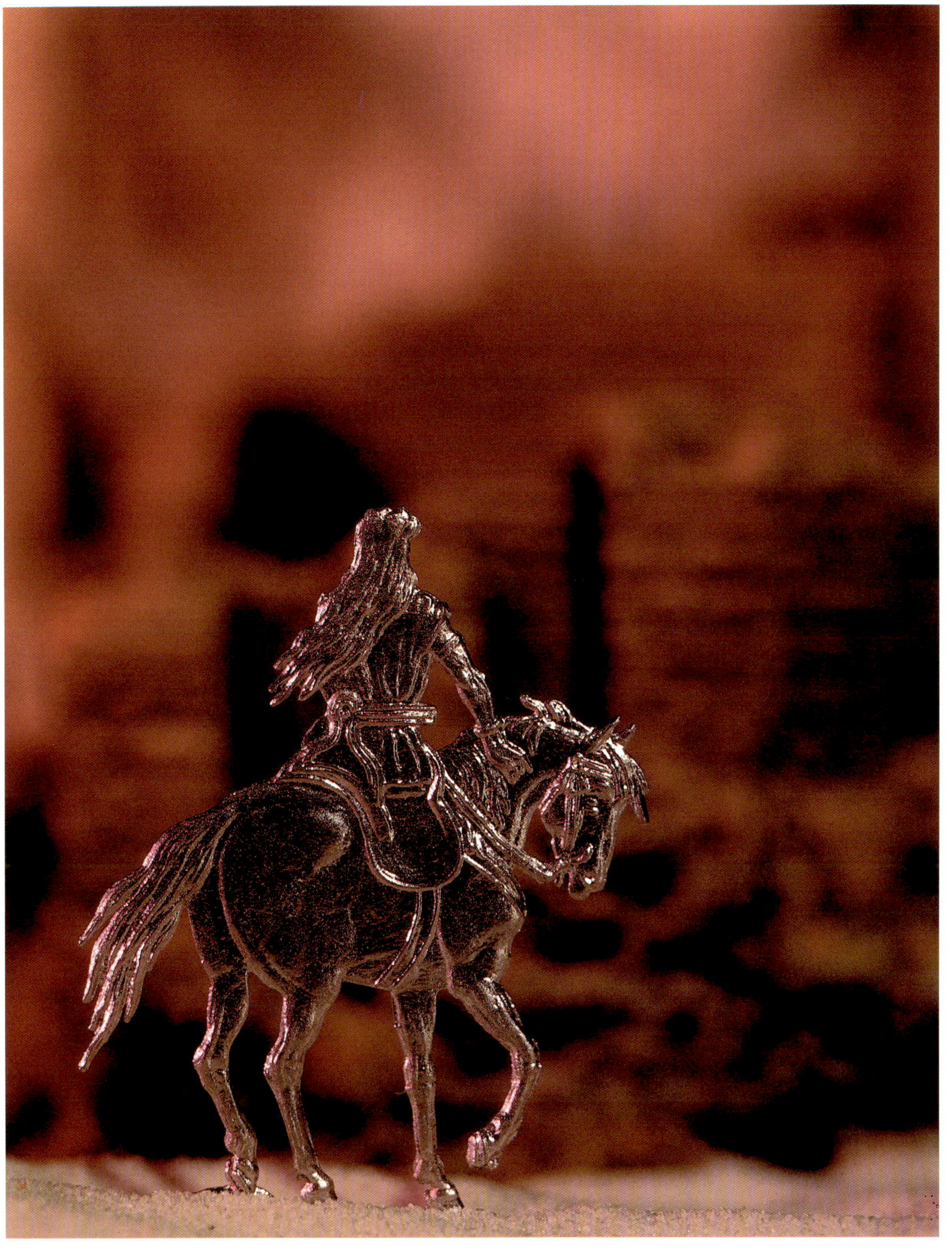

7. The Rhine Maidens
Die Rheintöchter
Cibachrome Print
1993

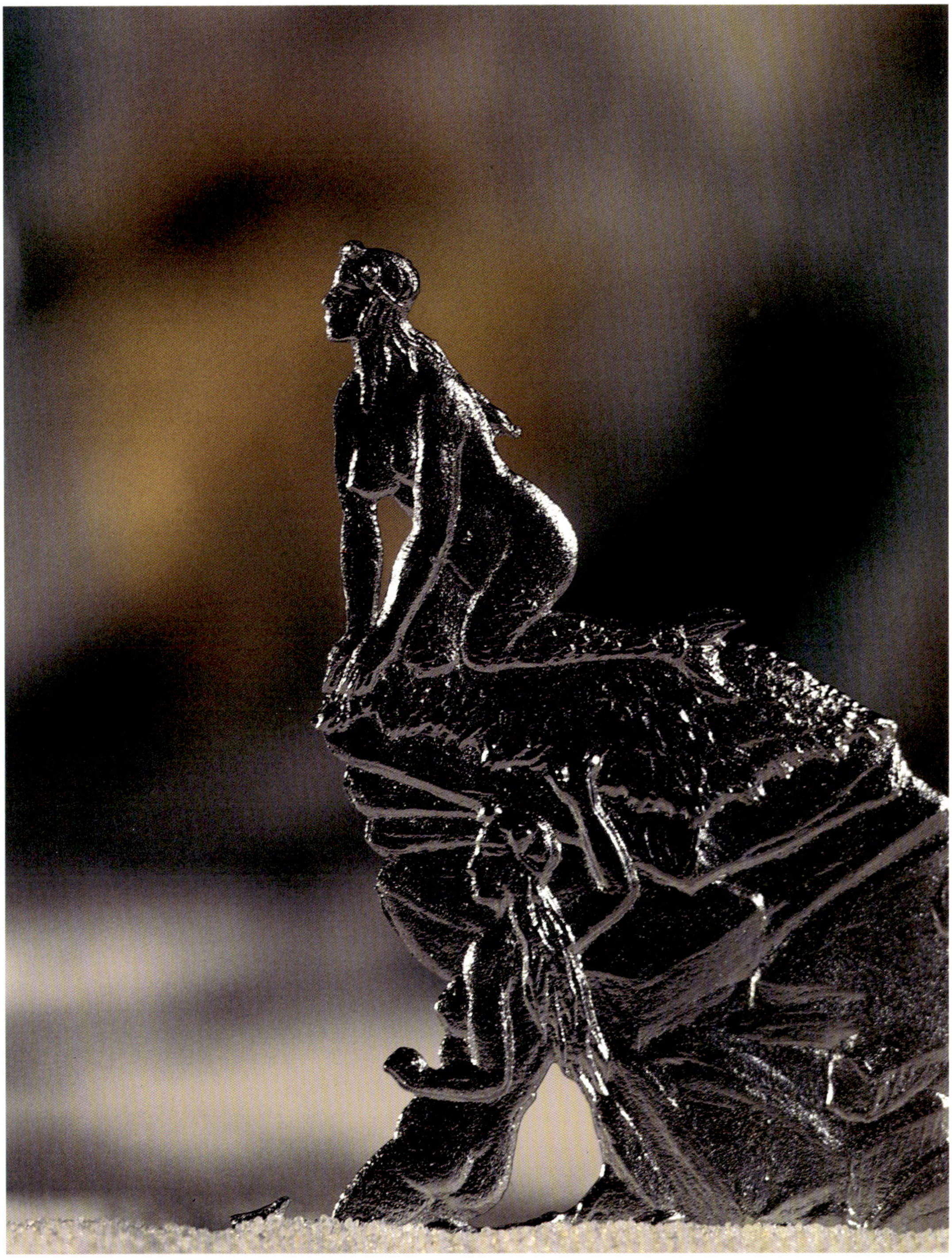

8. Hagen and Gunther
Hagen und Gunther
Cibachrome Print
1993

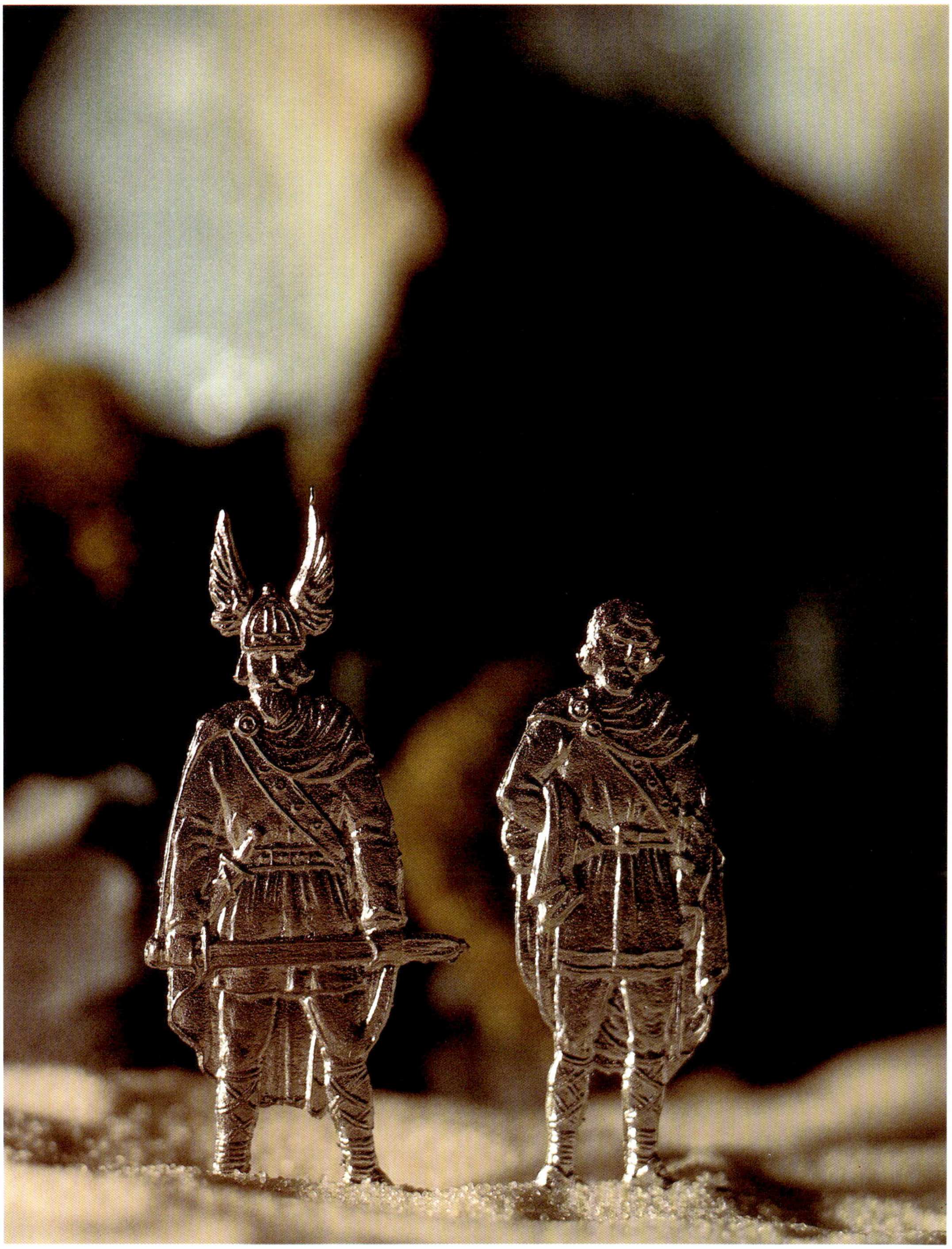

9. Kriemhild holding
Hagen's head aloft
Kriemhild hält
Hagens Kopf hoch
Cibachrome Print
1993

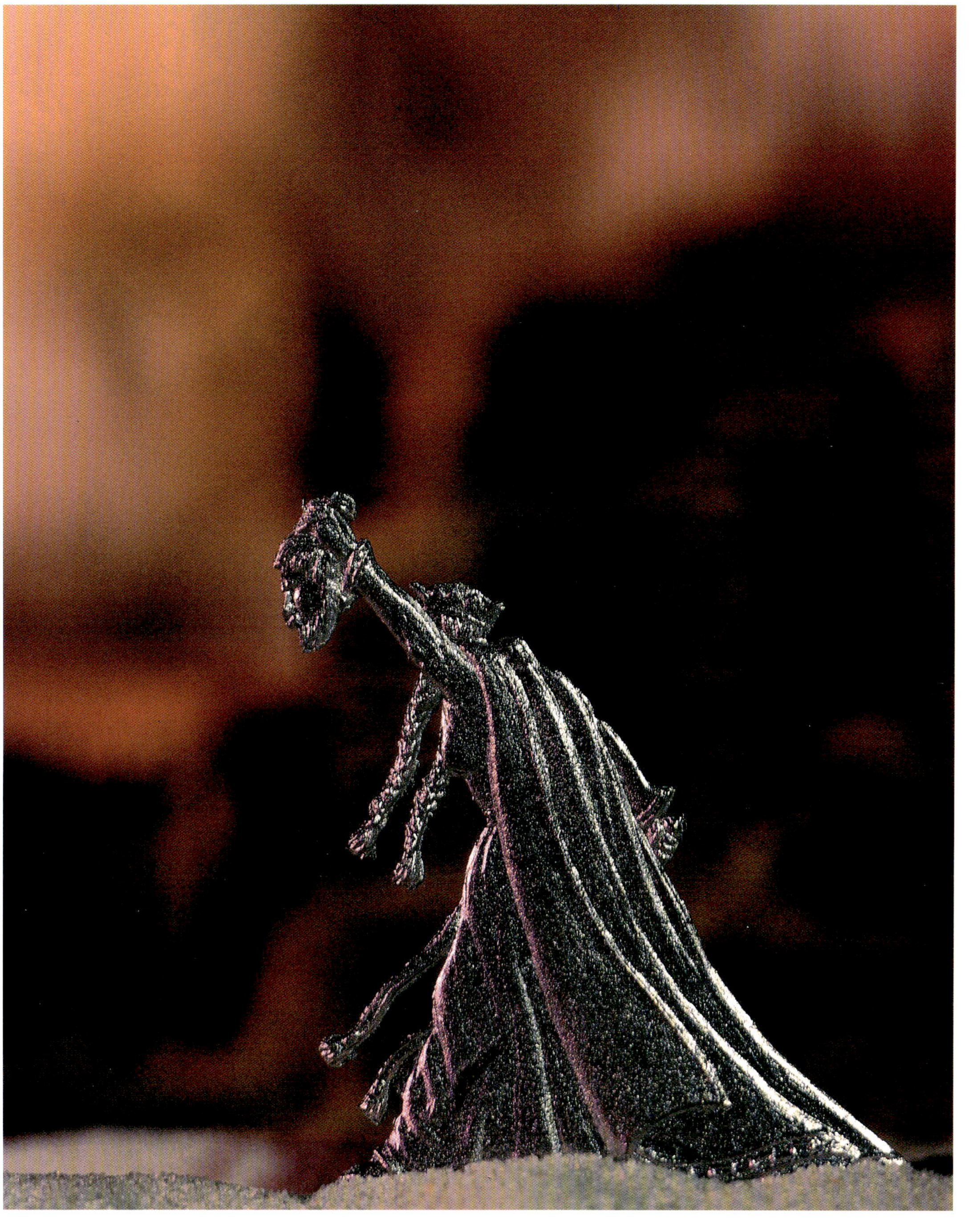

Biography

David Levinthal

Born: 1949, San Francisco, CA.
Lives and works: New York, NY.

Education:

1981 S.M. Management Science, M.I.T.
1973 M.F.A. Photography, Yale University.
1970 A.B. Studio Art, Stanford University.

Selected Solo Exhibitions:

1993 Galerie H.S. Steinek, Vienna, Austria.
Wiener Staatsoper, Vienna, Austria.
The Friends of Photography, Ansel Adams Center, San Francisco, CA.
Southeastern Center of Contemporary Art, Winston-Salem, NC.
Laurence Miller Gallery, New York.
1992 City Lites Gallery, Tokyo, Japan.
1991 Janet Borden, Inc. New York.
Jack Glenn Gallery, Los Angeles, CA.
Laurence Miller Gallery, New York.
Museum für Gestaltung, Zürich, Switzerland.
Forum Böttcherstraße, Bremen, Germany.
1990 Pence Gallery, Santa Monica, CA.
Laurence Miller Gallery, New York.
1989 University Art Museum, California State University, Long Beach, CA.
Jan Kesner Gallery, Los Angeles, CA.
1988 C.E.P.A. Gallery, Buffalo, NY.
Laurence Miller Gallery, New York.
Clarence Kennedy Gallery, Polaroid Corporation, Cambridge, MA.
Allied Arts Gallery, Las Vegas, NV.
1987 303 Gallery, New York.
Philadelphia College of Art, Philadelphia, PA.
1986 University of Alabama, Birmingham, AL.
Blatent Image Gallery, Pittsburgh, PA.
1985 Area X Gallery, New York.
Founders Gallery, University of San Diego, CA.
1978 International Museum of Photography at George Eastman House, Rochester, NY.

Quivera Gallery, Albuquerque, NM.
1977 Carpenter Center of Visual Arts,
Harvard University, Cambridge, MA.
California Institute for the Arts, Valencia, CA.
Southern Light Gallery, Amarillo College, TX.

Selected Group Exhibitions:
1992 "More Than One Photography,"
Museum of Modern Art, New York.
"Sofort-Bild-Geschichten",
Museum Moderner Kunst, Vienna, Austria.
"Interpreting the American Dream," James Casebere, David Levinthal, Richard Ross. Galerie Eugen Lendl, Graz, Austria.
"Illusions et Travestissements,"
A.B. Galerie, Paris, France.
1991 "Devil on the Stairs," Institute of Contemporary Art, Philadelphia, PA, Newport Harbour Museum, CA.
"Des Vessiers et des Lanternes," La Botanique, Brussels, Belgium, Palais de Tokyo, Paris, France.
"Recent Acquisitions,"
Amon Carter Museum, Fort Worth, TX.
1990 "Odalisque," Jayne Baum Gallery, New York.
"Rethinking American Myths,"
University of Connecticut.
1989 "Surrogate Selves:
David Levinthal, Cindy Sherman, Laurie Simmons,"
The Corcoran Gallery of Art, Washington D.C.
"Photography of Invention," National Museum of American Art, Washington, D.C.
"The New Concept," Forum Stadtpark, Graz, Austria.
"The Mediated Imagination,"
SUNY Purchase, New York.
"Abstraction in Contemporary Photography,"
Hamilton College, Clinton, NY.
"Constructed Realities," Kunstverein, Munich, Germany.
1988 "The Return of the Hero," Burden Gallery, NY.
"The Constructed Image II,"
Jones Troyer Gallery, Washington D.C.
"Selections 4," Photokina 88, Cologne, Germany.
1987 "Avant-Garde in the Eighties,"
Los Angeles County Museum of Art, CA.
"Fabrications,"
International Center of Photography, New York.
"Photography and Art 1946-86,"
Los Angeles Couty Museum of Art, CA.
1986 "Acceptable Entertainment,"
Bruno Faccetti Gallery, New York.
"Signs of the Real," White Columns, New York.
1985 BC Space, Laguna Beach, CA.
1983 "In Plato's Cave,"
Marlborough Gallery, New York.

Selected Public Collections:
Museum of Modern Art, New York.
Art Institute of Chicago.
Amon Carter Museum, Fort Worth, TX.
BankAmerica Corporation, San Francisco, CA.
Corcoran Gallery of Art, Washington, D.C.
Georgia Museum of Art, Athens Georgia.
Grand Rapids Art Museum, Grand Rapids, MI.
Hallmark Collection, Kansas City.
High Museum of Art, Atlanta, GA.
International Museum of Photography at
George Eastman House, Rochester, NY.
Los Angeles County Museum of Art.
Museum of fine Arts, Houston.
Museum of Contemporary Photography,
Columbia College, Chicago.
National Gallery of New Zealand, Wellington.
New York Public Library.
Norton Gallery, West Palm Beach, FL.
Polaroid Collection Cambridge, MA.
The Brooklyn Museum, New York.
University Art Museum, California State University,
Long Beach, CA.
Milwaukee Art Museum, WI.
The Minneapolis Institute of Arts.
Birmingham Museum of Art, Alabama.
Eurostar, Graz, Austria.
Continental Insurance, New York.
Progressive Art Collection, Mayfield Heights, OH.

Selected Bibliography

Aletti, Vince. "Valley of the Dolls," The Village Voice, May 21, 1991, p.95.

Barnes, Lucinda. Centric 35: David Levinthal, California State University Long Beach, 1989.

Berry, Wendell. "Property, Patriotism and National Defense," Aperture: The Return of the Hero, Spring 1988, pp.32-40.

Brooks, Rosetta. "A Biennale of Our Own," 7 Days, May 3, 1989, p.24.

Brooks, Rosetta. "David Levinthal: American Beauties," Laurence Miller Gallery, N.Y. and Pence Gallery L.A., 1990.

Carlson, Lance. "Enlarging the Photographic Impact," Artweek, April 29, 1989, p.12.

Coleman, A.D. "New York City as Subject and Inspiration," The New York Observer, January 9, 1989, p.12.

Coleman, A.D. "The Image in Question," Center Quarterly Vol.9, No.4. Summer 1988, pp.4-9.

Costello, Michael. "Tabletop History," Afterimage, April 1978, pp.18-19.

Deville, Francoise and Alain D'Hooge. Des Vessies et des Lanternes. Bruxelles; Les Editions du Botanique, 1991.

Eauclaire, Sally. "Hitler: A Chronicler of Horror," Rochester Democrat & Chronicler, February 19, 1978, pp.1E,4E.

Faber, Monika. "Sofort-Bild-Geschichten," catalogue, Wien, Museum Moderner Kunst, 1992.

Fox, Howard N. "Avant Garde in the Eighties," Los Angeles County Museum of Art, 1987.

French, David. "Seeking Critical Dialog," Artweek, November 28, 1987, p.6.

Goodmann, Tim. "Absolutely Successful," Palo Alto Weekly, August 16, 1989, Sec.2, pp.29-30.

Grunberg, Andy. "Where Blurred Focus Makes Sharp Statements," The New York Times, December 20, 1987, Sec.2, pp.39, 42.

Grundberg, Andy. "Image and Idea," The New York Times Magazine, Part 2, August 30, 1987, pp.74, 117.

Grundberg, Andy and Kathleen McCarthy Gauss. "Photography and Art Interactions Since 1946," New York, Abbeville Press, 1987.

Heiferman, Marvin and Carol Kismaric. "Getting Close to Gotham," ARTnews, September 1987, pp.106-111.

Hirsch, Robert. "Exploring Colour Photography," Dubuque, Iowa, William C. Brown Publishers, 1988.

Hoy. Anne H. "Fabrications: Staged, Altered and Appropriated Photographs," New York, Abbeville Press, 1987.